STO

ACPL ITEM
DISCARDED

4

THE FIRST BOOK OF THE MOON

THE FIRST BOOK of

THE MOON

BY CARROLL V. GLINES COL. U.S.A.F.

FRANKLIN WATTS, INC.
575 Lexington Avenue
New York, N.Y. 10022

Jacket photo: Close-up of Mare Imbrium region. Courtesy, U.S. Air Force, Cambridge Research Laboratories, Hanscom Field, Bedford, Mass. Technical Photo Branch.

SBN 531-00586-0

TO
KAREN, KEYES, DAVID, AND VALERIE

Contents

THE FIRST BOOK OF THE MOON

Introduction

FOR MANY CENTURIES men have looked toward the heavens at night and wondered about the ever-changing yet changeless yellow-white globe that moves across the sky. Sometimes men have also seen it in the daytime and tried to figure out what it was doing there chasing the sun.

There were some men who were more curious than others. They would keep records of the moon's comings and goings, what it looked like on certain days, and how it seemed to affect the ocean tides, harvests, animals, and people. This curiosity, plus the fact that the actions of the moon could be predicted in advance, caused many ancient peoples to reckon time in larger units than just a day. The moon's changes in its *phases* — from new to full, and back to new again — defined the original "month" and thus helped men devise the first calendars. One of the days of the week, Monday, was derived from the belief that the second day of the seven-day cycle was sacred to the moon (the "moon's day") while Sunday was the "sun's day."

Today the moon occupies the attention of curious men of the world, just as it has through the centuries. The American people have committed themselves to the national goal of sending men to land on and explore the moon in the near future. Hundreds of scientists are laboring to learn as much about space flight and the moon itself as they can before our astronauts brave the hazards of such a flight. Men *will* go to the moon. Only the exact time of their going remains uncertain.

Why do we want to send a man to the moon? What possible advantage can there be in going there if it is a "dead world," without water, vegetation, air, or any form of life? How much do we *really* know about the moon? How will men get there? Could there be

1

some truth to the many myths and superstitions that have been handed down through the centuries? These are just some of the questions that are being asked today as brave men prepare to go to that celestial body — and beyond. These questions and many more will be answered in the pages that follow.

From Fancy to Fiction to Fact

OVER TWO THOUSAND years ago, a Greek philosopher named Philolaus made this statement: "The moon is similar to the earth. It is inhabited as our earth is, and has larger animals and more beautiful plants than our earth affords. The animals on the moon are fifteen times stronger than those on earth [because] the days on the moon are fifteen times longer."

Philolaus could not prove his assertions, but he is credited with being one of the first men in history to write about the moon and have his words preserved for posterity. However, Philolaus was not the first man to believe that there was life there, for the ancient Greeks, who lived hundreds of years before his time, believed that the spirits of their important statesmen lived on the moon in perpetual happiness. The earliest moon-fiction story, written by Lucian of Samosata, was titled *Icaromenippus* and was concerned with such a voyage to the moon by Menippus, the hero of the tale.

It is perhaps the Babylonians who should get credit for being the first people to be scientifically curious about the moon. Their cities, situated along the banks of the Tigris and Euphrates rivers, had cloudless skies most of the year. On the highest hills surrounding the cities, tall brick watchtowers shaped like pyramids were built. An open platform was placed on top, where the astronomers of the day recorded their observations about the moon and stars on small clay tablets. Many of these tablets, some dating as far back as 3800 B.C., have been found in ancient ruins and represent some of the oldest written records ever found.

2

While the Babylonians made their observations in a scientific way, their interpretations of what they saw became the basis for many of the ancient myths that developed. Actually, these men were not really scientists, but priests, and each observation was a sacred rite. The observation towers were religious temples. The sun, moon, and stars were gods and goddesses who held the power of life and death over earthly mortals. The astronomer-priests believed that everything that happened on earth could be predicted in advance, for it was revealed in the skies. Thus, no undertaking of any importance was ever made without consulting the heavens through the astronomer-priests. So influential were these men in Babylonian life that no battle was fought, no ship launched, no crops planted, no business transacted, and no journey begun without asking their advice. These men, taking advantage of the riddles of the universe and the ignorance of the times, were virtual rulers because they were able to distinguish between a good omen and a bad one — the latter foretelling a disaster to an individual or a nation. The very word *dis-aster* means "bad star."

It was not long before the record-keeping Babylonian astronomers realized that there was a definite pattern to the comings and goings of the moon and the sun. The sun gave an easy reckoning for the days. But longer periods of time had to be reckoned so that they could account for the seasons and determine the right time to sow crops and reap the harvests. The phases of the moon provided this larger unit of time measurement because there was a complete cycle every twenty-nine or thirty days. From this measurement of time was derived the word "month" from "moon," because the word "moon" actually means "to measure."

The Babylonians also discovered that twelve moon cycles seemed to coincide with the cycle of seasons as governed by the movement of the sun. Thus, a year was decided upon which would be 365¼ days in length. However, the twelve lunar months totaled only 354 days since it was found that the moon cycle was 29½ days. Thus, at intervals decided upon by the astronomers, an extra month was added to make the solar and lunar calendars come out even. This thirteenth month was considered a time of bad omens and the astronomer-priests were in great demand at this time for counseling. In fact, the number 13 is still considered by some to be an unlucky number.

After the year and the month had been settled, even shorter units of time were needed. One-fourth of a month became the time period known to us as a week, and this, in turn, was divided into seven days. The day was then divided into twenty-four parts called hours. The daylight hours were measured with a sundial, while the nights were measured by burning a marked candle or using an hourglass which allowed sand to drop through a small opening at a regular rate. But, while this combination of scientific observation and superstition did contribute to human progress, the heavens themselves were still considered mysterious and fearsome.

Just as the words "month" and "Monday" have been derived from "moon," so have other familiar words which still connote the fears and beliefs of ancient peoples. The words "lunatic" and "lunacy" were originally coined to describe a kind of insanity — with occasional lucid intervals — which was supposed to be influenced by the changes of the moon. A disease of horses, known as "moon blindness," was also supposed to be caused by the moon because it occurred at regular intervals. "Moonshiners" are so-called because they distill illicit "moonshine" spirits by the light of the moon. And, a person was said to be "moonstruck" if he had a mental disorder which seemed to be allied somehow with the phases of the moon.

The Babylonian belief in the mysticism of the heavens was shared by the Egyptians, the Hindus of India, the Chinese, the Maya of Mexico, the American Indians, and, of course, the Greeks. In

4

their various ways, these peoples all worshiped the bright objects that seemed to move across the sky. Each culture had its beliefs which led, in turn, to classic stories which were handed down from generation to generation.

The Greeks perpetuated the most famous of such classics. The sun god was Helios who awakened each morning and drove his golden chariot pulled by four white horses across the sky. Selene was the sister of Helios and was the goddess of the moon (moon geography today is called *selenography*). She was supposed to have ridden her chariot across the heavens at night and ruled the night skies until Helios awakened in the morning.

The legends and myths persisted during Roman times. In 160 B.C., a part of Cicero's *Republic*, entitled "Somnium Scipionis" ("Scipio's Dream"), presented a conception of the whole universe; it was the first presentation of the notion that the earth was relatively insignificant compared to the rest of the universe. Moreover, it was the first known written work in which the vastness of space was visualized, and in which appear "stars which we never see from earth."

For centuries after Lucian's story of a flight to the moon, no further stories of space travel appeared. Then, in the sixteenth century, an Italian poet named Ariosto published *Orlando Furioso* in which a character named Astolpho went to the moon in a chariot. Astolpho found the moon to be a "rich champagne," with open countryside and many earthlike cities and towns.

Since there was still no specific information about the moon, one writer's imaginative work on the subject was as good as another's. It was the Italian scientist Galileo who was the first to change fiction into fact. In his quest for something with which to see the moon better, he invented what he called an "optick tube," in the winter of 1609-10, and pointed it toward the golden glow in the night sky over Italy. Although Galileo's telescope was primitive

5

The Italian scientist Galileo and a drawing of his "optick tube."

by today's standards, it gave him a spectacular view of the lunar surface never seen by anyone before.

News of Galileo's telescope spread quickly. In that same year, 1610, perspective cylinders — as they came to be called — were brought to England. There Sir William Lower claimed the distinction of being the first Englishman to look at the moon through one. That same year, too, Galileo published his *Siderus Nuneius*, in which he described the moon as a "world of mountains and chasms and contrasts of blinding light and total shadow." He then drew the first maps of the moon, thus marking the true beginning of a scientific study of the moon using an instrument that supplemented man's eyesight.

Galileo believed that there was no atmosphere or water on the moon. However, Johannes Kepler, a German astronomer, wrote in his book *The Mysterious Cosmos* that it was possible that the moon

6

was not a waterless, airless body, and that its movement caused the tides in the oceans of the earth. Kepler clarified the mathematics of the planets and formulated three important laws of planetary motion:

1. *The planets travel in elliptical orbits with the sun at one focus;*

2. *A line drawn from a planet to the sun sweeps over equal areas in equal times, which means that the speed of a planet varies. It travels faster when it is closer to the sun and slower as it moves away;*

3. *The squares of the periods of revolution of any two planets are proportional to the cubes of their mean distances from the sun.*

Kepler had read the revolutionary theory of Nicolaus Copernicus, the great Polish astronomer — that the earth revolves around the

The German astronomer, Johannes Kepler, discoverer of the laws of planetary motion.

7

The English scientist, Sir Isaac Newton.

sun (not vice versa) — and agreed with its logic. But Kepler went one step further in his analysis of the Copernican theory. He wrote that "the sun not only stands in the center of the universe, but is its moving spirit. My aim is to demonstrate that the celestial machine is rather like a clockwork in which a single weight drives all the gears, and that the totality of the complex motions is guided by a single magnetic force."

Another scientist who added to the sum total of man's knowledge in the seventeenth century was Sir Isaac Newton, who spelled out the laws which have become known as the laws of motion and gravity. Newton explained the nature of the sun's force when he formulated his "universal law of gravitation," published in 1687 as the *Principia*. This law recognized that the force of gravity is a universal force in the sense that every particle in the universe is attracted to every other particle by a force that is proportional to the sum of their masses and is inversely proportional to the square of the distance between them. It is this basic principle that explains why the moon revolves around the earth while the earth and the other planets revolve around the sun.

For the first time, by putting this knowledge together, the behavior of the planets and all other bodies moving in space was explained. It was these three scientists — Galileo, Kepler, and Newton — who did more in a short period of time to push back the frontiers of man's knowledge about the moon than all those who had preceded them. They bridged the gap between fancy and fact and made the first giant step toward fulfilling the dream of centuries — that men would someday actually set foot on the moon.

Birth of the Moon

IN SPITE OF our vast knowledge about the planet on which we live, scientists have not been able to determine exactly how the earth was formed. Many theories concerning its formation have been advanced, but so far, no one has been able to offer enough scientific proof to support one particular theory. It is therefore understandable that we know even less about the moon, which is the earth's satellite and our nearest celestial neighbor.

It has been estimated that the earth was formed more than four and a half billion years ago. This estimate is based on the fact that the age of the oldest rocks in the earth's crust can be fairly well calculated. Many such rocks contain radioactive materials, such as uranium, which decay at a steady rate into lead. Since this rate of decay is known, the extent to which the original uranium decays provides a guide to the time that has elapsed since the rocks solidified. The moon is believed to have been formed at approximately the same time but, of course, until the elements on its surface can be analyzed, no one can do more than guess.

One of the many theories concerning the origin of our solar system is called the *nebular hypothesis*, originated in 1796 by a French mathematician named Pierre Simon de Laplace. The La-

THE NEBULAR HYPOTHESIS

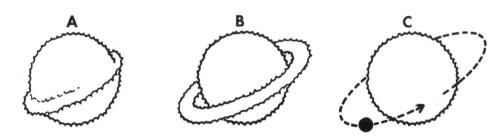

How a planet was formed according to Laplace's nebular hypothesis. Stages show ring being formed and flung off from central mass, then condensing into a solid planet. One such ring was supposed to have become the moon.

place theory — not now accepted — held that the solar system began as a vast cloud of tenuous, or loosely composed, gas. Over a long period of time, the cloud was supposed to have shrunk and thrown off rings. Each ring, in turn, was condensed into a planet and the sun was formed as the main residue of the original cloud. The earth, as one of these newly formed bodies, was then supposed to have thrown off a ring of gas of its own which in time became the moon.

Later, scientists rejected the Laplace hypothesis and newer theories developed. Some of these were based on a "gravitational incandescent gas" theory or "the theory of the wandering star" where a celestial body was supposed to have passed close by the sun and attracted a "tongue" of matter. This subsequently broke up into "drops" which formed the planets.

Still another theory concerning the origin of the moon is known as the *tidal hypothesis*. It was first propounded by Sir George H. Darwin, son of the great naturalist Charles Darwin. The younger Darwin first assumed that the earth and moon had been one body and

10

that the moon had been thrown off as a fluid mass due to the wobbly, unstable orbit of the main earth mass. While round at first, the earth later became elliptical due to two huge forces acting upon it — the tides caused by the pull of the sun and the vibration caused by its own revolutions. Darwin reasoned that there was a period of time when the earth's tides increased to such an extent that it caused the original earth mass to become first pear-shaped, then the shape

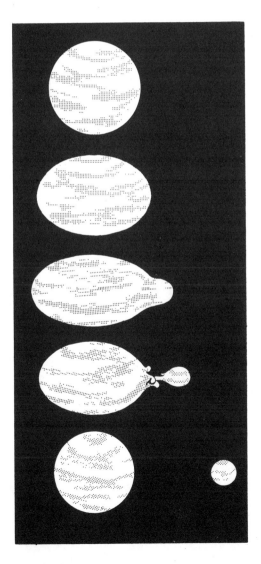

Darwin's tidal theory of the moon's formation. Theory assumed that moon was thrown off the earth while the earth was in an unstable equilibrium, as shown in the drawing. Once the weight of the moon's mass was gone, earth was supposed to have gone into a stable orbit around the sun, with the moon then revolving around the earth.

of a bowling pin. Finally, the neck of the "pin" broke off and the top of the "pin" was thrown into orbit. As a result of this break, both the earth and the moon regained their spherical shapes as they orbited about the sun.

There were many scientists who adhered to the tidal theory, for it received much support from the American astronomer W. H. Pickering. Pickering accepted the Darwin theory, but went one step further. "Look at a map of the earth's surface," Pickering's argument went, "and you will see that the lands on the opposite sides of the Atlantic Ocean would fit into each other if they were placed together. The 'body' of Africa would fit into the hollow of South America, and the eastern coast of North America roughly corresponds to the western coast of Europe. The great area of the Pacific, then, is the great rounded hollow from which the moon was pulled. The continents on the opposite side of the earth broke away and slid into their present positions. The moon could thus have originated in the vast area now covered by the Pacific Ocean, the earth's largest body of water."

Most present-day scientists do not subscribe to this tidal theory. Their disbelief in it is based on the mathematical argument that a mass as large as the moon could not have been hurled into space, as Darwin and Pickering supposed, simply because it is too big. Instead, modern scientists generally believe that the moon did *not* originate as a piece of the earth and that the earth-moon system should be considered as a double planet rather than a planet and a satellite.

Yet another theory concerning the moon's origin is the *particle accumulation theory*, which holds that the moon and the earth, along with the rest of the solar system, grew by the gradual accumulation of solid particles of matter. Thus, according to this theory, the cloud of gas from which the earth and moon came consisted of solid particles instead of hot gas. When the particles within the

12

cloud collided, they tended to stick together, much as particles of snow stick together to form a snowball. Slowly, the ball of particles collected more and more particles, sweeping the solar system almost clean of smaller particles as the larger bodies circled the sun.

It is still not known whether the moon and the earth were formed together. However, there is general agreement that the moon became a satellite of the earth soon after the two bodies were formed, if not at the same time. But, no matter what their origin, or when, we do know from radioactive dating methods that both the earth and the moon were probably formed more than 4.5 billion years ago.

The answer to the question of how the moon was formed may remain a mystery for many years to come. It is ironic that after hundreds of years of looking at, and studying, our nearest neighbor in space, we are still uncertain how it got there. Someday, perhaps in our own lifetime, scientists will find out the truth.

The Changing Face of the Moon

MEN OF ANCIENT TIMES must have been baffled by the constantly changing face of the moon. They must have wondered why it changed from a thin crescent to a round dish of light, and then changed back again to a crescent. For centuries it was believed that the moon, the sun, and all the stars revolved around the central earth. Since they appear to do so, this was certainly a natural assumption to make; but today, of course, we know that this is not so.

The first man to question this basic assumption was Aristarchus of Samos, a Greek philosopher who suggested in the third century B.C. that the sun and not the earth was the center of our planetary system. As is so often true of those who think differently and dare to challenge basic assumptions, Aristarchus was laughed at and he found few followers. Later, philosophers lapsed into the old earth-centered theory. Chief among these men was Claudius Ptolemy, who wrote a massive book called *The Great Astronomical System*. For centuries this work dominated scientific thinking about the movements of the earth and celestial bodies. Ptolemy's system was necessarily complicated because he sought to explain the irregularities in the movements of the sun, moon, and planets he observed. Yet his reasoning seemed logical and he found many supporters. He wrote that these irregularities can be explained "by uniform circular motions, because only such motions are appropriate to their divine nature." Although it is now known to be wrong, Ptolemy's system did enable astronomers to predict the future positions of the heavenly bodies with an accuracy never before known.

The first recognized challenger of the Ptolemaic theory was a Polish churchman named Nicolaus Copernicus, who published his own conclusions in *On the Revolutions of the Heavenly Spheres* in 1543. Copernicus had learned Greek in order to study the writings of the early Greek astronomers. He had not been convinced that Ptolemy had adequately explained all of the irregularities of the heavens and he was surprised that several of Ptolemy's contemporaries agreed with him. He studied the writings of Aristarchus, who had first claimed that the earth moved instead of the sun. "From this," Copernicus wrote, "I conceived of the earth's motion, and I myself began to meditate upon the mobility of the earth." His basic theory was summed up in these three paragraphs:

> *Of the moving bodies, first comes Saturn, who completes his circuit in thirty years. After him, Jupiter, moving in a twelve-year revolution. Then Mars, who revolves once every two years. Fourth in order an annual cycle takes place, in which is contained the Earth, with the lunar orbit as an epicycle. In the fifth place, Venus is carried around in nine months. Then Mercury holds sixth place, circulating in the space of eighty days.*

14

The Polish churchman and astronomer, Nicolaus Copernicus.

In the midst of all dwells the Sun. And so, as if seated on a royal throne, the Sun rules the family of planets as they circle about him.

We find, therefore, under this orderly arrangement, a wonderful symmetry in the universe, a harmonious relationship in the heavenly motions which cannot possibly be obtained in any other way.

The book Copernicus had written did not arouse unusual interest at the time largely because few accepted his theory. Anyone with "common sense" could see that the sun and the moon moved from east to west and that the earth did not move beneath one's feet.

But not everyone thought Copernicus was crazy. Galileo, when he was a young mathematics professor at the University of Padua in Italy, adopted the teaching of Copernicus because "his point of view explains to me many things which certainly cannot be explained by the commonly accepted [Ptolemaic] view." He had written this in 1597 in a letter to a friend, but added: "I have dared not publish my views, frightened by the fate of our teacher, Copernicus, who acquired immortal fame with some, and yet is an object of ridicule and derision to an infinite multitude of others — so great is the number of fools."

With the aid of the telescope that he had built and perfected, Galileo discovered that, contrary to the teachings of Ptolemy and other earlier investigators, not all of the heavenly bodies shone with their own light. While stars such as the sun were self-luminous, the planets were like the moon; they could only reflect the light of the sun. Galileo also discovered that the Milky Way was really a cluster of stars instead of clouds; that Jupiter had moons of its own; and that the sun was undergoing constant change through cataclysmic eruptions on its surface.

The Movements of the Moon

THE MOON'S MOVEMENTS are obviously associated with the phases of the moon. Since the moon has no light of its own, it "shines" only by reflecting the light it receives from the sun. It revolves around the earth from west to east in 27 days, 7 hours, and 43 minutes. At the same time, the earth is revolving around the sun; this journey takes 365 days. Because the moon rotates once each time it circles the earth, the same half of the moon is always turned toward us.

Although it may appear to do so, the moon does not really change its shape. The sun can light up only one half of the moon at a time, just as it does the earth. Once a month the sun, earth, and moon are in this position:

Earth   Moon   Sun

At this time we cannot see the unlighted side of the moon. However, two weeks later the moon is on the other side of the earth:

Moon   *Earth*   *Sun*

The people on the dark side of the earth see the entire moon lighted. It is "full" at this time, while at other times a lesser portion is lighted until the sun's rays are directly behind it and it cannot be seen from the earth.

Various phases of the moon are caused by changes in relative position of the sun and moon as moon revolves around the earth. While half of the moon is always lit by the sun (except during lunar eclipses), only when it is in position 3 is the entire sunlit half visible from earth. At other times, only lesser portions of the sunlit side can be seen from earth. At the position of new moon, it cannot be seen until it moves again toward position 1.

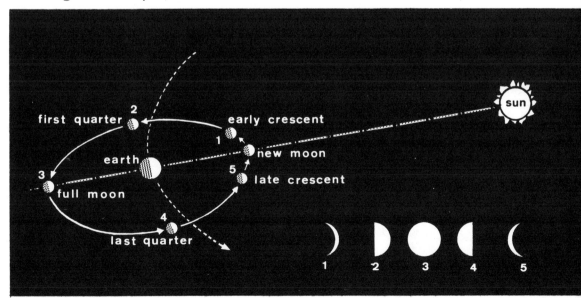

While it takes 27⅓ days for the moon to revolve around the earth, the cycle of phases from one new moon to the next takes 29½ days. During the 27⅓ days that the moon is making its circuit around the earth, both the earth and the moon are moving around the sun. The distance the earth moves in that time accounts for the extra two days required for the phases of the moon to complete one cycle.

Eclipse of the Moon

THE EARTH, the sun, and to some extent all of the other planets in the solar system have a gravitational effect upon the moon. The earth, of course, has the strongest effect since it is nearest. Both the earth and the sun try to force the moon to move in an orbit that is in line with each of their equators; however, since the planes of both these equators are not exactly in line, these two forces are constantly pulling and pushing. The result of these forces on the moon is such that the gravitational effect on it is constantly changing.

If the path of the moon around the earth were a perfect ellipse, the earth would pass between the sun and the moon, causing a *lunar eclipse* once each month. Similarly, the moon would pass between the sun and the earth once a month to cause a *solar eclipse*. But the ever-changing, irregular orbital course of the moon prevents the three bodies from being in a direct line very often. Therefore, eclipses involving the moon are rare.

A total eclipse of the sun — when the disk of the moon completely darkens the sun — is an exciting event for astronomers. They will travel many miles to a spot on the earth's surface where the moon will be directly between the earth and the sun. This is an important scientific event because it is at such times that the sun's atmosphere can best be studied. Since the moon appears just large enough to cover the sun at this time, the "belt of totality" (where

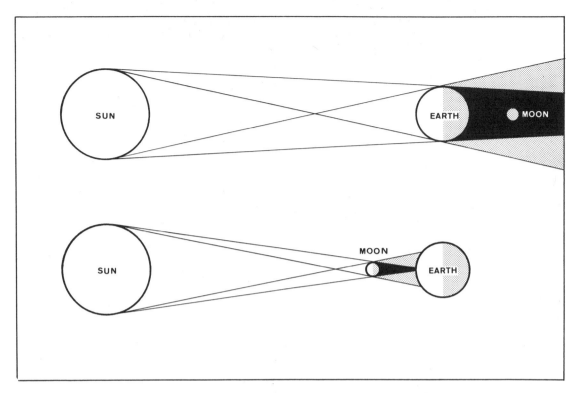

Above: A lunar eclipse occurs when the moon passes through the earth's shadow. Below: Passage of moon between the earth and the sun causes a solar eclipse.

the eclipse appears to be complete on the earth) is always narrow — no more than 170 miles at any one time.

Not only is an eclipse of the moon seen more frequently on earth but it can also be viewed from more points on earth than can a solar eclipse. In fact, it is visible from a complete hemisphere of the earth because it is caused by the earth's shadow passing in front of the moon as shown in the accompanying illustration.

Not all lunar eclipses are total eclipses. Sometimes they are partial and other times they are *penumbral,* which means that the moon only dims because it does not pass into the *umbra,* or total shadow, of the earth.

19

Photo above shows a total solar eclipse. Bottom photo shows a lunar eclipse, but not a total one. An eclipse such as this is called an annular eclipse — one in which the moon's disk does not completely cover the sun. Annular eclipses are of special interest because they permit very precise measurements of the shape of the moon. Also, heights of valleys, mountains, and ridges can be measured. (Photo above, courtesy NASA; photo below, courtesy U.S. Air Force)

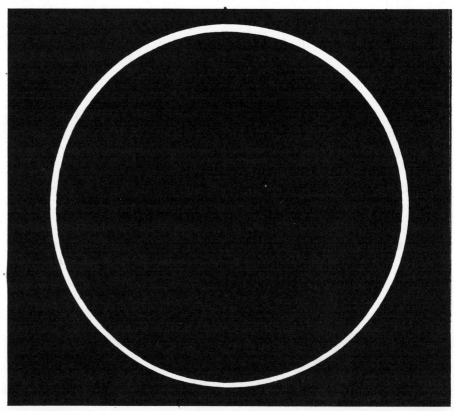

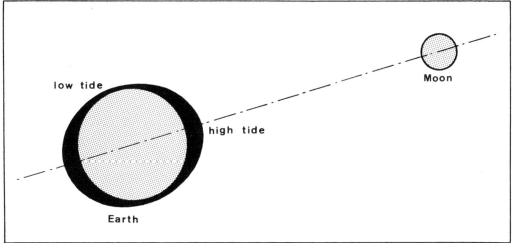

Simplified drawing shows how moon's gravitational pull influences ocean waters on the earth's surface, causing tides.

The Tides

THE MOON affects the earth in several ways. The principal one is the phenomenon which causes the *tides,* or rising and falling of the earth's oceans. As the moon moves around the earth, its gravitational force attracts the great bodies of water, literally pulling them away from the earth in a giant bulge. This great ocean swell follows the moon around as it makes its daily trip. At the same time, because the solid portion of the earth is also affected by the moon's gravitational pull, a second tidal effect is formed on the side of the earth opposite the moon.

Strange as it may seem, what we normally think of as the solid body of the earth is also affected by the moon, so that it, too, has a tide. The landmass of the earth is elastic and actually rises and falls about 4½ inches. We do not feel these land tides, but they do take place. Of course, this is much less than the waters of the ocean, which rise and fall many feet.

In addition, there are tidal effects acting on the earth's atmosphere, which are also caused by the moon. The atmospheric layer above the earth, called the *ionosphere*, reflects and therefore can

21

relay radio messages for great distances between points on the earth's surface. It is now believed that the moon also causes "tides" in the ionosphere which, in turn, may influence radio reception. It is possible that the moon influences the earth in other ways as well. For example, a few scientists have tried to correlate earthquakes with the phases of the moon and have found that many earthquakes have occurred when the moon is full. The moon is also thought to have an influence on the weather, but neither of these influences has yet been proved scientifically.

Lunar Composition and Structure

IT HAS BEEN ESTIMATED that the density of the moon is about $3\frac{1}{3}$ times that of water. The density of the earth, on the other hand, is $5\frac{1}{2}$ times that of water. Therefore, it follows that the moon is made of lighter material than the earth.

Scientists know from spectroscopic analysis of the light coming from the stars that all of them are made up of similar basic elements, although they may be in different proportions. Thus the moon could have many of the elements that the earth has, except for one or more of the heavier materials. The earth's center is believed to have a large core made up of an iron-nickel compound. It is possible that this heavy material is lacking on the moon. Meteorites which strike the earth seem low in iron content.

The internal structure of the moon is as much a mystery as the material that composes it. The question which must be answered is whether or not the moon's chemical composition was ever so hot that it was molten. If it was, its interior should exist in layers, with the heavier elements having settled toward the center. If it was never molten, then its composition would be much the same throughout.

The Moon's Craters, Rays, and Seas

WHEN THE MOON is viewed through a telescope, its most striking features are the large number of craters which pockmark vast areas of its surface. Some of them are small pits a mile or so across, while others have a diameter of 140 miles or more. There are many thousands of craters on the side of the moon that we can see.

Moon geographers, or selenographers, have estimated that the walls of some of the observable craters are 15,000 feet above the floors. One of them, Newton's Crater, has a depth of 30,000 feet. All of them are basically circular in shape, and they are all shallow in relation to their diameters. Although the craters away from the center of the moon appear as ovals, this is only an optical effect due to the fact that we cannot look directly down into them. Thus they appear to us as ellipses; but by studying them under all possible angles of illumination, scientists know they are, without exception, circular.

The largest craters are probably the oldest. They were most likely formed when the moon was being "born." Today, however, they are badly worn down and broken. In fact, selenographers call them *walled plains* because they are now no more than enormous barren fields characterized by deep gorges, ridges, chasms, and pits.

All of the major craters have been given names for easy identification by selenographers. Many of them have peculiarities and characteristics that set them apart from others. For example, Newton's Crater, located near the moon's south pole, is one of the deepest and probably the most desolate of them all. Because of its great depth and location, neither the earth nor the sun could be seen by a person standing on its floor. And, since it lies in an extremely rough area, it will probably be one of the most difficult areas to explore.

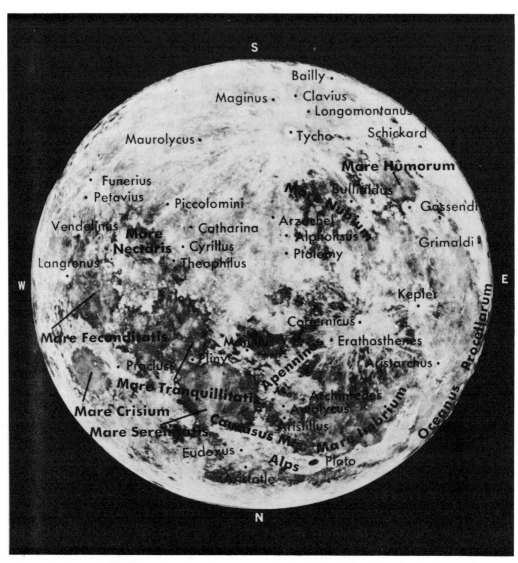

Some of the moon's more prominent seas (maria), *craters, and mountain ranges are indicated on this photo of the full moon as it is seen through an inverting telescope.* (Lick Observatory)

The crater Copernicus on the moon. Sometimes called "the Monarch of the Moon," it measures about 56 miles across. (Lick Observatory)

Other "name" craters are Theophilus, Alphonsus, Ptolemaeus, Copernicus, Tycho, Pythagoras, Kepler, Thaetetus, Bailly, Clavius, Cyrillus, Archimedes, Aristillus, and Autolychus. Of all these, selenographers have selected Copernicus, located on the Oceanus Procellarum, as the most typical and descriptive crater of all. It has been called "the Monarch of the Moon" because of its imposing appearance and the fact that it is probably studied more than any other single crater.

The crater Copernicus has walls that tower 17,000 feet above the "inner amphitheater." Measured across, from crater edge to crater edge, it is about 56 miles. However, when measured across the floor, it is only 40 miles because of huge landslides which have occurred at some time in the past.

The central area of Copernicus is made up of three major masses. Many smaller hillocks and mounds cover most of the floor so that it is by no means as smooth as it may look through a low-powered telescope. Other features of Copernicus are the "terracing" of the inner walls, the gentle slopes of the outer sides, and the many ridges and valleys that radiate away from it. From all appearances, it seems as if rivers of molten lava might have cut river-like gorges on the outer sides as they flowed into the surrounding plains. At present, however, scientists can only speculate on how any of the moon's topography was formed. The way these same phenomena occurred on earth might not be true for our nearest neighbor in space.

As telescopes became more powerful, and as moon photography became better, astronomers could see more and more details on the lunar surface. Where many parts of it looked smooth before, observers can now say that practically the whole surface of the moon is pitted with thousands of "craterlets" ranging in size from a few feet to more than ten miles across. And, just as the large craters on the great lunar plains tend to be aligned in chains, so do the craterlets.

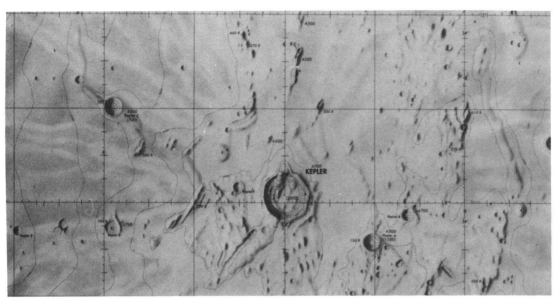

*Details of two moon charts, showing region of Kepler crater (above),
and region of Copernicus crater. (NASA)*

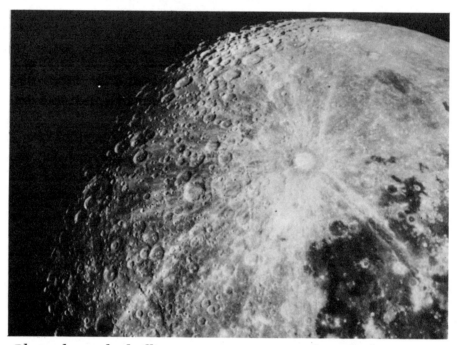

Photo shows the brilliant ray system surrounding the lovely crater Tycho. Crater was named after the great astronomer Tycho Brahe, a mentor of Johannes Kepler and one of the best naked-eye observers who ever lived. (U.S. Air Force)

One of the great mysteries of the moon, which baffles those who study it, is the bright *rays,* or lines, that emanate from many of the craters. Seen best at full moon when the sun shines directly on them, the rays look like bright lines that have been painted right across the craters, valleys, and seas. They cast no shadows, which leads scientists to believe that they are really deposits of minerals of some sort that have become exposed during the moon's millions of years of existence. The largest and most brilliant network of rays surrounds the crater Tycho.

While the craters attract the most attention, it is actually the moon's "seas" (called *maria* from the Latin word *mare,* meaning "sea") that cover most of the visible lunar surface. They are not really

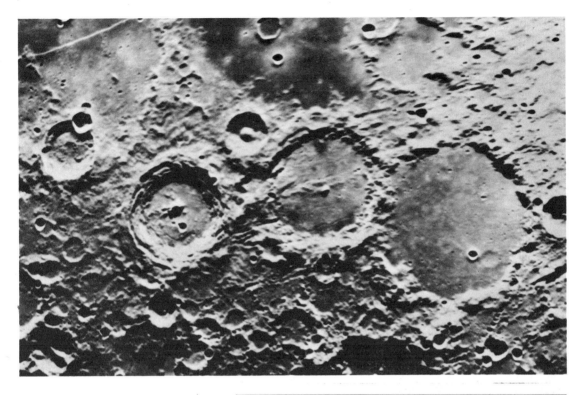

Photo above shows the crater Alphonsus (center). Lower photo shows close-up view of the same crater as taken by Ranger 9 camera. Floor of Alphonsus reveals intricate pattern of ridges and rills (cracks). Photo was taken 35 miles above the lunar surface, 23 seconds before impact. Point of impact is circled in white. (Above, courtesy U.S. Air Force; below, courtesy NASA)

seas at all, but vast darkish plains, which contrast immediately with the lighter craters when we look at the moon with the naked eye.

There are nine major seas and many minor ones. Since astronomers are still using Latin names for the "water" areas, the official name for the Sea of Vapors, for example, is *Mare Vaporum*; the Sea of Showers is *Mare Imbrium*; and the Sea of Nectar is called *Mare Nectaris*.

There are also "oceans," "bays," "lakes," and even "swamps" on the moon, all with Latin names. These terms probably stem from the belief that the plains might all have been molten lava at one time, and the fact that from the earth they *do* often look like bodies of water. However, most scientists do not believe that any form of water as we know it ever covered these areas of the moon. In any event, there is little doubt today that these lunar seas do not contain any form of liquid. They are probably dry plains or deserts — areas without a trace of moisture or any substance in the liquid form.

How Did the Craters Originate?

ANYONE LOOKING at the craters on the moon would be tempted to think that they were produced by ordinary volcanic action, similar to that on earth. However, volcanic mountains are raised above the earth's surface and have the shape of cones with small cup-shaped craters at the top. Lunar craters, on the other hand, are shallow depressions in the lunar surface, around which are heaped piles of lunar debris, forming rims.

Those who accept the volcanic concept say that the lunar craters were not the result of ordinary earthlike volcanoes but are structures called *calderas*. Calderas are caused when molten material beneath the surface is blown violently into the atmosphere; however, these are relatively rare on earth. When they do occur, the

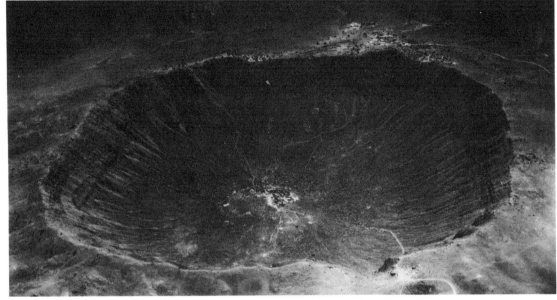

Meteor Crater, Arizona. (American Museum of Natural History)

molten material beneath the crust of the surrounding ground disappears and the ground on top collapses into the empty space to produce a shallow depression much like the lunar craters.

The other theory as to the origin of the lunar craters is called the *meteoritic theory*, which says that the craters are really the result of the high-speed impact of meteorites. The Meteor Crater in Arizona is the best example of these craters on the earth. It is 4,150 feet in diameter and was originally about 550 feet deep with a rim height of at least 150 feet.

Those who follow one or the other of these two popular theories of crater origin generally agree that craters with broad, smooth floors, such as Archimedes, Plato, and Ptolemaeus, were at least partially flooded with molten material at some time during their history.

The Lunar Atmosphere

SCIENTISTS are fairly certain that there is no atmosphere on the moon. At least there should not be unless there are gases surrounding the moon that are unlike any of the gases known on earth. Of course, no one will know positively until lunar atmospheric samples are taken by the first men to land there.

The reason scientists do not believe there is any atmosphere on the moon is based on the known velocity of gases when heated. Under the heat of the sun during the daytime on earth, the molecules of gases build up an ever-increasing speed. Any object (including molecules) on earth that builds up a velocity of seven miles per second can escape from the earth's gravitational pull. Fortunately, our vital earth gases do not reach this speed and so are not lost. On the moon, however, a velocity of only one and one-half miles per second is needed for escape, which is less than the velocity of hydrogen at the temperatures found there. Thus, over a period of millions of years, all gases surrounding the moon, if any ever existed in the first place, would have vanished into space, leaving a complete vacuum at the lunar surface.

There are at least two other reasons why scientists do not believe there is such a thing as a lunar atmosphere. During lunar eclipses, astronomers have noted no fuzziness or obscuring of the edge of the moon, which might be caused by atmospheric gases. When the eclipse is at its maximum darkness, light would "leak" around the moon's edges and its shape would be indefinite because the gas molecules would bend and dull the sun's rays if any such molecules were present.

The other reason is related to the first. When the moon is viewed in all its phases, there is no diffusion or scattering of sunlight on its surface. The lunar features are clear and sharp. Any diffusion is

This balloon-borne telescope, used by the U.S. Air Force to study the moon, is carried aloft by plastic balloons to 80,000 feet or more, where lunar observations are unobscured by the earth's atmosphere. (U.S. Air Force)

caused, not by the moon's atmosphere, but by the earth's as the astronomers try to pierce the latter's crust of gases, smoke, haze, and moisture. It is because of this problem that astronomers try to get their telescopes above most of the earth's atmosphere by putting them into balloons, satellites, and, someday, spacecraft. It is also for this reason that most astronomical observatories are located on mountaintops and away from populated areas.

The question of whether there are or are not any atmospheric gases on the moon is not as clear-cut as one might want to believe. There are a few scientists who believe that there is evidence of a "trace" of atmosphere there which might be made up of heavy gases whose molecules do not move rapidly when heated. These men say that it is possible that the inert gas argon might be present which would be the product of the decomposition of radioactive potassium in the lunar rocks. Two other inert gases, xenon and krypton, might also be clinging to the lunar surface, according to at least two eminent scientists.

Since the invention of the telescope, astronomers believe that they have occasionally observed patches of smoke or vapor, which they cannot explain, covering certain familiar lunar features. If so, it is possible that there are gases lurking in the many deep lunar crevices into which the sun never shines. Such gases might be frozen and resting there as solids until they are slowly melted and then vaporized. The heavy gases might conceivably be seeping out in small clouds, only to be eventually lost in space as the molecules are heated and their escape velocity is increased.

A situation closely allied with the subject of the moon's atmosphere — and a very important one to lunar explorers — is the effect radio waves will have there. As we know, a layer of charged particles called the ionosphere surrounds the earth at a varying altitude of from 50 to 400 miles. These electrically charged particles cause radio waves to be bounced back to earth so that radio signals can be sent around the world instead of being lost in space. If this were not possible, radio signals could only be transmitted relatively short distances between points on the earth's surface.

But what about radio signals on the moon? Could two moon explorers, miles apart, converse by radio if they were not in sight of each other? If there is an ionosphere similar to earth's there, there may be no problem; if not, many radio stations may have to be set up or communications satellites launched into moon orbit in order for explorers to talk to one another.

There is a slight bit of evidence that there may be a very thin ionospheric layer around the moon due to the distortions of signals received from lunar probes. For example, on September 13, 1959, the Russians sent Lunik II toward the moon and followed its radio signals until it crash-landed on the surface; it was the first man-made object to reach that goal. Before it crashed, scientists noted strange distortions of the signals which may have been caused by electrically charged gases. Lunik II was equipped to study cosmic rays, magnetic fields, and meteoric particles. It was reported that the number of ionized particles Lunik II encountered increased markedly about 6,000 miles from the moon.

The search for the scientific truth about the moon will go on. The study of the moon's atmosphere is but one of the many subjects that must be thoroughly studied with instruments before man will go to see for himself.

The Moon's Surface

SINCE NO MAN has yet been able to get a sample of lunar rock to analyze, we do not yet know what makes up the moon's crust. Scientists have calculated that the moon has a density index of 3.3, which means that it weighs 3.3 times more than an equal globe of water. It so happens that most of the rocks on the earth (called granitic rocks) are also of about the same density. However, it cannot be concluded that the moon consists of the same rocklike material. Indeed, most scientists think that the lunar surface is made up in part of a large layer of dust particles. A few, however, now believe that it is a loose layer of fine sandlike material from two to ten feet deep.

Much investigation of the moon's surface has been done in the last few years with radio telescopes. These are really instruments which measure the wavelengths of light waves which are beyond the visual capability of the human eye. For example, we cannot see infrared light because it appears black to the human eye. We cannot see X rays, yet they can be measured by instruments, and have been harnessed so as to be of immense value to mankind.

The 150-foot dish antenna at Stanford University, Palo Alto, Calif. (NASA)

So it is with radio waves, which, like light waves, can be focused, intensified, and measured. By the use of radio telescopes, scientists can study radio signals sent from earth and reflected from the moon. Like waves of light, radio waves can take "fingerprints" of the matter through which they pass or from that which sends them out. Although still very much in the experimental stage, *radio spectroscopy*, or the study and analysis of radio waves, will enable astronomers to obtain valuable information about the moon that cannot be obtained from optical telescopes.

It has been estimated that the moon reflects only about 7 per cent of the light it receives from the sun. Comparing this with the known rocks on earth, the nearest type of rock reflecting the same amount of light is *basalt*, a heavy substance of volcanic origin. However, this does not prove anything definite either, because some portions of the moon reflect more light than others.

Astronomers have analyzed the light reflected from the lunar surface and have found that some of the brighter areas are yellowish, rather than white, in color. Some areas have a greenish or grayish tinge, but the color difference is so slight that, indeed, there is some disagreement on whether there are any color differences at all, except that which may be the result of shadows or the slant of the sun's rays. However, recent investigations have found evidence in spectroscopic photographs that shows the existence of an element which may have two carbon atoms in its molecule. It is entirely possible that the colors, the occasional appearance of smoke or haze, and the detection of these carbon particles may all be related in some way.

Lunar Temperatures

PROBABLY ONE OF the most significant physical characteristics of the moon is its surface temperatures. Near the equator of the moon, temperatures will vary from over 200° F. in the daytime to 240° F. *below zero* at night. At the *terminator* (the line dividing the light and dark regions), and at the poles, the average temperature is about 60° F. below zero.

How do we know about the moon's temperature variations? Ingenious astronomers combined the telescope and a heat-measuring device, called a *thermocouple*, which is so sensitive that it can measure the heat emitted from an ordinary candle 6,000 miles away. Since the moon reflects light, a small amount of heat is also reflected and received on earth, although it certainly cannot be measured by any ordinary thermometer. The thermocouple, focused at various spots on the lunar surface, gives us reasonable estimates of the tremendous temperature differences. These will probably be found to be fairly accurate when men reach the moon.

Since there is such a wide temperature difference on the moon, it can only be assumed that, whatever the material is that makes up the surface, it does a poor job of retaining the heat once the sun's rays cease to shine on it. This is one more piece of evidence that the surface may be dust- or sandlike, because rocks, as we know them, tend to retain heat much better than that. However, *pulverized* rocks also react in this way.

The lack of an atmosphere on the moon prevents the transfer of heat across the lunar surface from one area to another. Therefore, an explorer will find great extremes of temperature even in daylight. If he walks from a lighted area into a shadow, and then back into the light again, he may have undergone a change of 200 degrees in a period of a few seconds.

Although we tend to think of the back of the moon as dark, and therefore extremely cold, this is not so. The side of the moon we cannot see is lighted by the sun when our side is dark; therefore, the temperature variations should be just as great there — although we cannot yet measure them.

So far, the lunar temperatures that have been determined are representative only of the surface. It is believed that because the lunar material is a poor conductor of heat, the temperature a few inches below the surface may be relatively steady at about $-20°$ F. While this is still uncomfortable from our standpoint, this knowledge may be useful to the moon explorers. Lunar bases may be located underground to protect explorers from the tremendous heat differences while they sleep. They would also be protected against any cosmic rays and meteorites they may encounter.

The Other Side of the Moon

ONLY ABOUT 59 PER CENT of the moon's surface can be seen from the earth. This is because the same side of the moon is always facing the earth. For centuries astronomers have wondered what the re-

38

maining 41 per cent that cannot be seen looks like. The fact that they could not devise any scientific method to find out has caused much anxiety and speculation. It has even sparked poems such as this one by an anonymous poet:

> *O Moon, lovely Moon with the beautiful face,*
> *Careening throughout the bound'ries of space,*
> *Whenever I see you, I think in my mind —*
> *Shall I ever, O ever, behold thy behind?*

It remained for Russian scientists to be the first to answer the age-old question. On October 4, 1959, two years after they successfully orbited the first man-made satellite around the earth, the Soviets launched Lunik III toward the moon. Its main function was to pass beyond the moon, photograph the far side, and transmit photographs back to earth. The flight was a successful one. The world's scientists waited breathlessly, and on October 24, several photographs were released. They were of poor quality but provided a first look at all but about one-eighth of the far side.

These photographs have been studied carefully and it is believed that the surface on the opposite side is relatively unbroken as compared with the side we can see. There seem to be fewer deserts, craters, and mountains. This has tended to give more credence to the theory that the gravitational pull exerted by the earth on the moon may have caused a disruption of the near-side crust and is, therefore, the reason for the volcano-like craters. However, even these pictures cannot be called conclusive. The sun was at its zenith when the photographs were made so that there were very few shadows to enable astronomers to study the contours of the surface. More and better pictures must be taken at different times and these pictures compared closely before we will know definitely about the back side of the moon.

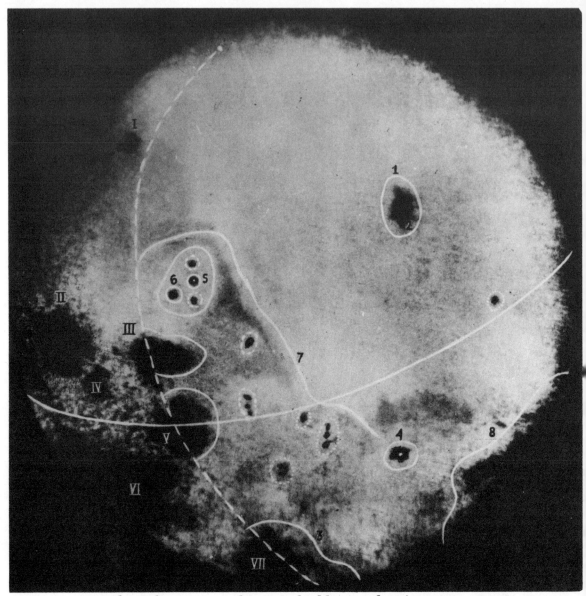

Far side of the moon as photographed by Lunik III's camera. Numbers refer to physical features as follows: 1. Sea of Moscow. 2. Gulf of Astronauts in the Sea of Moscow. 3. Continuation of Mare Australe on back side of moon. 4. Tsiolkovsky crater. 5. Lomonosov crater. 6. Joliot-Curie crater. 7. Sovietsky mountain range. 8. The Sea of Dreams. Roman numerals refer to continuations of physical features on the visible side of the moon, as follows: I. Mare Humboldt. II. Mare Crisium. III. Mare Marginis. IV. Sea of Waves. V. Mare Smythii. VI. Mare Fecunditatis. VII. Mare Australe. (Sovfoto)

Before releasing the Lunik III pictures, Soviet astronomers picked out the most prominent landmarks they could identify and gave them names. A depression north of the lunar equator, estimated at 180 miles across, was named the "Sea of Moscow," and a feature in the same area has been named "The Gulf of Astronauts." Other names honored Mikhail V. Lomonosov, whom the Soviets credit with designing the first helicopter; Joliot-Curie, a French Communist nuclear scientist; and Konstantin E. Tsiolkovsky, a Russian space pioneer who died in 1935.

The Russians have made a chart of the far side of the moon and have identified 498 formations. There still remains a region that has not been photographed, but this will probably be done in the near future. Better pictures will be made and better maps drawn. The day will surely come when the far side will be as familiar as the side that men have seen for thousands of years.

Life on the Moon

IS THERE ANY LIFE on the moon? Not as we know it here on earth. The living things as we know them — insects, animals, plants, human beings — could not exist on the moon's surface. The extremes of temperature, the lack of oxygen, and the lack of minerals and foods would not permit earth-type living things to survive even a few seconds.

Our scientists, however, remind us that since the earth is only one small planet in a limitless universe, it is possible that there may be some sort of life on the other planets of the solar system or their moons.

The moon, as we have seen, is not at all like our earth. We are reasonably sure that there are no two-legged or four-legged animals roaming about on its surface. But what about the lower forms of life — bacteria, worms, small plants, or mosses?

41

Scientists have asked — and are still asking — that same question. And they seem almost unanimous in their opinion that absolutely no form of any living organism can live on the moon's surface. However, there are a few who do not rule out the possibility that some form of life may exist beneath the lunar surface. The speculation that gases may be present inside the moon and that temperatures are fairly constant a few inches under the crust leave this possibility open to argument.

There are more scientists who believe that life *may* have existed on the moon millions of years ago than will say that it exists there now. If the lunar seas once contained water or some liquid, marine life might have survived until the liquid dried up.

Of course, we will not know whether there was any life on the moon until the first men land there. Those first explorers will gather lunar rock, dust, and air samples, and earth scientists will analyze every minute speck, searching for the answers to the questions of centuries. What they will find we do not know. All we know now is that brave men *will go* and *will* return with more knowledge than we now possess.

Mapping the Moon

EVER SINCE telescopes were invented, astronomers have made maps of the moon. This was done so that they could easily refer to the familiar landmarks and provide an atlas for the preservation of the names they gave to those features. Since it has been possible to boost man-made objects out of the earth's gravitational field into space and onto the moon, maps of the lunar surface have become very important. As the day gets closer when explorers will take a first-hand look at the moon's surface, they will need accurate maps in order to orient themselves and navigate on and over that surface.

42

Moon cartographers will tell you that the job of moon-mapping is not easy. The moon is devoid of many of the natural features which serve as checkpoints on earth. There are no forests, stretches of meadowland, bodies of water, or sandy desert areas. There are mountains, of course, although the longest range of them extends only a little more than 400 miles.

Because the moon is only about a quarter of the earth's size, the horizon will always be closer to an astronaut. Astronomers estimate this distance at perhaps 2 miles or less. This shortening of the horizon will deny a lunar explorer a chance to take a "fix" on more distant surface features of sizable elevation because these will be below his line of vision. The sharper curvature of the lunar surface may also make an explorer's portable radio useless after about 2 miles. Some authorities estimate that even a 100-foot antenna atop the lunar vehicle or at base headquarters would only boost the effective range of a radio to something like 12 miles.

It is because of these conditions that our lunar explorers will have to depend heavily upon maps for guidance. Although many astronomers have described the moon's surface as a monotonous wasteland — sometimes it has been likened to portions of the Badlands in the Dakotas — it does contain numerous topographical features which an astronaut can match against those shown on the moon charts. Using these, he can pinpoint where he may land and in what direction any planned exploration should take him. These features are depicted on a scale of 1:1,000,000, with shaded relief, contours, and tones representing color variations.

Should the landing be in the vicinity of a crater such as Kepler, the astronaut will be able to establish his position by relating it to the other craters which exist in the same vicinity. Kepler, incidentally, happens to be one of those craters with a ray system — long, broad, light-colored streaks of unknown composition which radiate from the crater walls like the multiple spokes of a wheel. A moon

An aerospace technologist checks a chart with lunar landscape on this planetarium demonstration machine. (NASA)

explorer, studying his chart, could determine, for example, which ray to follow to get to an area specified by his mission. It should also be noted here that scientists are still uncertain whether the moon possesses a magnetic pole, and if so, what its strength may be. For this reason, compasses cannot be depended upon as much as they can be on earth.

How these moon map-makers conducted this remote survey of a celestial body so far away is almost as fascinating as the first manned mission to the moon promises to be. For charting purposes, the earth's atmosphere is no friend of the camera. The densest innermost atmospheric layer, or troposphere, extends to mean altitudes of about 7 miles. Its air is usually unstable, subject to turbulence, and polluted by dust, smoke, and other contaminants. In the next layer — the stratosphere, whose arbitrary boundary ends some 22 miles out — optical conditions improve, but handicaps to photography still prevail. At far higher altitudes, as research satellites have found, cosmic dust and other celestial debris have also been encountered.

In photomapping the earth by high-flying aircraft, atmospheric turbulence and dust-fogged air are adverse factors, but pose no great problem. The aircraft operates at a relatively low altitude above a mapping area; fast photographic techniques and extraneous light sources make it possible to get clear, undistorted photographs from which accurate maps can then be made. In photographing the moon, however, the generally erratic behavior of the atmosphere and its changing clarity are major headaches. The intrusion of light from some other source can ruin a photographic plate. Moreover, the distances involved, all well over 200,000 miles, add to the exacting nature of the work. The greater the distance, the more exaggerated or distorted a photographic error can become. Air turbulence or contaminants may also cause small random variations in scale across the moon's image.

To bypass the densest part of the troposphere, photographs of the moon were taken at Pic du Midi, the loftiest observatory in the world. Built atop a peak in the Pyrenees in southern France, Pic du Midi is located slightly over 9,400 feet above sea level and is far removed from any city whose illumination might affect its telescopes. The air above high mountains is normally what astronomers describe as "still," and still air makes for "good seeing" by telescope.

Thus the problem of taking moon photographs so that landmarks can be accurately placed was solved quickly by the use of the Pic du Midi Observatory. But measuring elevations and identifying characteristics of other features so far away were not easy.

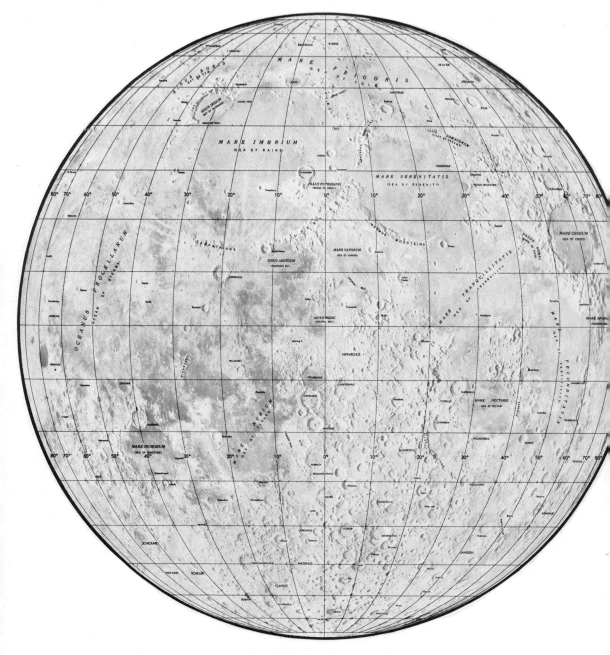

The U.S. Air Force's official map of the moon. (U.S. Air Force)

This difficulty was solved by using a shadow-measuring technique developed at the University of Manchester in England. Although the system dates back to the nineteenth century, it was refined and updated by a small group of students directed by Dr. Zdenek Kopan of the university's astronomy department, which was under contract with the United States Air Force.

Knowing the positions of the sun, moon, and earth, geometry is applied: by measuring the length of the shadows cast by sunlight, the elevations and depressions on the moon's surface can be determined.

Dr. Kopan obtained photos for this work by setting up a 35-mm modified movie camera. It took three exposures a minute of specific areas on the moon. The time-lapse photos show the changing shape of the shadow as it is cast on the moon's surface.

Over a two-year period, about twelve thousand individual photos of selected lunar regions were made. They were supplemented by other photographs from Lick and Mount Wilson observatories in California, the MacDonald Observatory in Texas, and the Yerkes Observatory in Wisconsin.

After many geometric calculations, cartographers have now given us a new conception of the topography of the moon. Contrary to the former concept of craggy cliffs and abrupt craters, most of the moon's surface is now found to be relatively smooth, with gently sloping hills and ridges.

Obtaining lunar photographs is only the beginning of compiling a chart of the moon. A visual observation unit has been set up by the United States Air Force to pick up with the human eye the detailed information missed by the camera lens. From a perch on a 300-foot mesa overlooking Flagstaff, Arizona, some 7,200 feet above sea level, Air Force personnel at the Lowell Observatory are busy painting the moon's portrait. In shifts, when the moon "poses" with its features in the best light, they observe it through the 24-inch refracting telescope and, on existing lunar photographs and drawings, make notes of what they see. They do this because photographs taken through the telescope do not always do as good a job as the human eye.

The earth's atmospheric turbulence makes any kind of viewing (either by camera or by human eye) difficult because of a constant shimmering effect which, in turn, makes this portrait-painting job a real chore. Sometimes, when the atmosphere "settles down," the image also calms down and "seeing" becomes clearer. Sharp "seeing" at its ultimate is rated at 10. No "seeing" at all starts at 0. On the best nights, features that normally are not visible are sharply defined, and the observer feels that if he puts his hand out he can touch that section of the moon on which his telescope is focused.

That is the way these observers work. They do not look at the moon's whole image at one time. Separate, small sections are brought into focus and observations of them are annotated on corresponding sections of photographs. The next day, these annotations are interpreted and airbrushed into the master shaded relief drawings. In this way, literally pore by pore, the moon's maps are being made.

As our nation's space vehicle operations require more and more detailed charts and aerospace navigation information, the challenge to map-makers will increase. More challenges will lead to more experience; consequently, wherever man plans to go on the lunar surface, the moon chart-makers are confident that they can, cartographically, precede him.

Trailblazers for the Explorers

WHILE THE MAP-MAKERS are busy gathering data for their maps, other scientists are seeking the answers to many other questions that must be known before men dare venture to the moon. Many un-

Photo at left was taken by Ranger 9 camera at an altitude of 12.2 miles, 8.09 seconds before impact in the crater Alphonsus. Large crater near left margin is situated on a shallow rill running upward. Right photo was last one taken before impact at an altitude of 4.5 miles above the lunar surface. (NASA)

manned, instrumented spacecraft will precede them. These craft will provide vital information about the moon's strange environment, help determine the best landing areas, and test many of the systems to be used for manned journeys.

A number of unmanned spacecraft have already gone moonward and have sent back valuable information. First were the series of Pioneer space probes. Then, on July 28, 1964, Ranger VII was blasted off Cape Kennedy, and 68½ hours later it crashed into the moon's surface. During the last 18 minutes of flight it took 4,136 extremely clear pictures and transmitted them to earth. The first pictures were taken about 1,600 miles above the moon. As Ranger VII fell closer and closer to the surface, smaller and smaller craters appeared on the pictures, and the very last picture to be transmitted was taken about 1,000 feet above the surface. Tiny craters, about a yard in diameter, could be detected.

Ranger IX, sent aloft in March, 1965, returned even better pictures and gave man his closest and sharpest look at his lunar neighbor up to that time. Aimed at the crater Alphonsus, it showed the known *rills* (cracks) more clearly than they had been seen before, plus many new ones. Alphonsus had been chosen as the impact point because its floor is level and it seemed like an excellent landing area for lunar explorers. Instead, it was found to be pitted with thousands of tiny craterlets, some showing dark halos.

Astronomers will study these photographs for a long time. Not only will they be of value to the lunar explorers but they seem to bolster the theory that the moon is of volcanic origin. The black-haloed craters are the main clues, plus the fact that the floor of Alphonsus seems to show evidence that loose lunar material has drained into underground cavities and cracks.

The Successful Mission of Surveyor I

WHILE THE RUSSIAN lunar probe program seemed ahead of that of the United States, the U.S. spacecraft Surveyor I, launched on May 30, 1966, clearly demonstrated American superiority in the race to the moon. Sent aloft from Cape Kennedy, Florida, atop an Atlas-Centaur rocket, the ungainly 620-pound space vehicle eased itself to a soft landing on the moon's Ocean of Storms (Oceanus Procellarum) 63½ hours later. Scientists on earth then radioed a command, and the craft's television camera began to take its first pictures. In the next twelve days, Surveyor I sent an amazing 10,338 photographs of remarkable clarity back to the craft's control center on earth.

Surveyor I's graphic pictures enabled scientists to draw their firmest conclusions yet about the moon's surface. It is the concensus of those connected with the program that the lunar surface is very similar to the earth's soil, with many substances that appear similar

Photo above shows engineers assembling NASA's Surveyor I space-craft for soft landing on moon. Below is an artist's conception of the craft and its gear in operation on the lunar surface. (NASA)

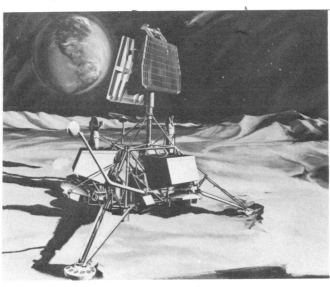

51

to our own rocks. The bearing strength is about 5 pounds per square inch, which means that the lunar surface will definitely support the weight of the first craft planned for a manned flight.

A color photograph taken by Surveyor I shows a rough-surfaced gray rock lying on brownish soil. This craft, in giving us our first close-up look at the moon's surface in color, has scored another "first" and has brought closer the day when astronauts will see for themselves what the moon is really like.

Surveyor I was equipped with more than 100 instruments, including temperature sensors, strain gages, accelerometers, and position-indicating devices. The results of their readings will be studied for many months. In addition, the three-legged spacecraft — actually an aluminum frame — was equipped with TV cameras, rotating mast, solar panels, fuel tanks, rocket engines, sensing devices, and guidance equipment. The fact that everything worked perfectly was a tribute to the ingenuity of the scientists of the United States.

This Surveyor I photo of the moon's surface was disturbed by the spacecraft's footpad. (NASA)

A wide-angle Surveyor photo of a cratered lunar surface southwest of spacecraft at low-sun illumination. Crater in center is about 11 meters from spacecraft and 3 meters wide. (NASA)

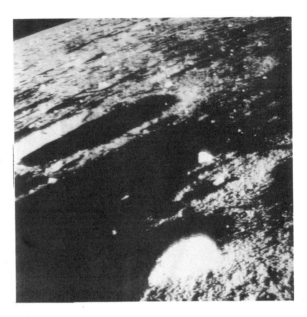

A narrow-angle photograph of the lunar scene southwest of the Surveyor spacecraft at low-sun illumination. Cratered surface is littered with blocks up to a meter or more in width. (NASA)

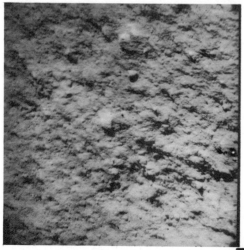

Close-up photo of moon's surface near Surveyor spacecraft, showing fine detail. Fragment in center is several centimeters long. Smallest grain that can be resolved is 1 millimeter. (NASA)

This Surveyor shot shows a line of large, rounded blocks in foreground which mark the rim of a large, ancient crater several hundred meters in diameter. Far rim of same crater can be seen on the lunar horizon. (NASA)

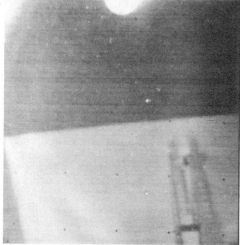

This Surveyor I photo of the lunar surface, transmitted to earth and received at NASA's Jet Propulsion Laboratory in California, shows a star constellation and the planet Jupiter. Planet is just above horizon at center of photo. Bright object at top is a latent image of the sun from a previous photograph. (NASA)

Here Surveyor's camera picks up small craters varying in width from a few centimeters to tens of centimeters, with particles and clumps of particles from millimeters to centimeters in width. (NASA)

A mosaic of Surveyor I photographs. (NASA)

In this Surveyor photo, sun's corona appears above lunar horizon shortly after lunar sunset. (NASA)

55

Scale model of the moon and NASA's Lunar Orbiter. Simulation shows how the unmanned, camera-carrying satellite is designed to approach within less than 30 miles of the moon to take high-resolution pictures. (NASA)

The Lunar Orbiters

IN ADDITION to the Surveyor series, a series of other craft called Lunar Orbiters will be sent into moon orbit to obtain photographs of the surface. These will aid in the selection of the best sites for later Surveyor spacecraft and the Apollo manned lunar expedition to follow. The Lunar Orbiters will also add to knowledge about the size, shape, and other characteristics of the moon.

Lunar Orbiter I, which was launched in August, 1966, became the first United States spacecraft to orbit the moon. It was the first orbiter ever to send photographs back to earth so that they could be seen on nationwide television. Although the pictures were not as good as was hoped for, many valuable lessons were learned.

Also, a series of satellites called Orbital Solar Observatories are aiming their instruments at the sun. Some of their information may contribute to the development of reliable methods of predicting solar flares, which can subject astronauts to deadly doses of radiation. A reliable forecasting system would make possible the scheduling of moon journeys that would avoid unsafe solar periods.

Other United States satellites and space probes will explore and monitor the space between earth and the moon. Their principal objective will be to help those first brave men to land on the moon and return — safely.

The Russians' Luna 9

WHILE THE UNITED STATES goes ahead with its unmanned lunar program, with full public disclosure of its failures and successes, the Soviet Union continues its exploration in great secrecy. After several failures in their Luna series, Luna 9 blasted off Russian soil on January 31, 1966, in a four-phase mission to place a television-reporting station on the moon.

The first phase put Luna 9 into orbit around the earth, and the second phase sent it into a lunar orbit. The third stage was a correction of the flight trajectory to ensure that the moon station would land in the pre-chosen Sea of Storms. The last and most difficult stage of all was the braking and "soft" landing on the lunar surface.

Luna 9 weighed 3,482 pounds and contained a television system which would ensure a 360-degree view and transmission of pictures back to earth. It landed on February 3, 1966, and began transmitting pictures about seven hours later. Although the Russians had wanted to release the pictures themselves, the radio telescope located at Jodrell Bank, England, intercepted the signals and released photographs of amazing quality a few hours later.

The Russian achievement of making a soft lunar landing was significant in itself but the photographs promise to answer many

The large radio telescope at Jodrell Bank, England. (NASA)

questions that have been puzzling scientists for generations. "No visible traces of dust are found on the lunar surface," a Russian scientist commented when he saw the photographs. However, American lunar geologists are not yet in agreement with this. Some say that the Luna 9 photographs show a glassy volcanic lava bed which proves that volcanoes have exploded over vast areas of the moon's surface and may still be active in some sectors.

The Stepping-Stones to the Moon

THE TWENTIETH CENTURY will be remembered hundreds of years from now for many things. Of all the technological progress made after 1900, historians may regard the most spectacular and important invention of all to be the rocket. The concentration and control of tremendous rocket power has enabled scientists to send instruments millions of miles into space and to transmit valuable information about the vast universe of which the earth is such an infinitesimally small part. Rockets have blasted many satellites into orbit around the earth, moon, Mars, Venus, and the sun. And human beings, not to mention dogs, monkeys, mice, and other animals, have been lofted into space and have been returned to earth safely.

Historians will give credit to the scientists of the Soviet Union for the first major breakthrough in the many steps that will be taken toward landing on the moon. On October 4, 1957, Sputnik I became the earth's first satellite and transmitted valuable data back to earth for three weeks before its batteries failed. On November 3, 1957, a dog, Laika, was sent into orbit for another Russian "first."

The sudden arrival of the space age prompted vigorous American interest in the new medium. On January 31, 1958, Explorer I was sent into orbit by the United States and discovered the inner Van Allen radiation belt; it also reported back valuable micrometeorite data. Since these successes, the race to the moon has been on in earnest, with the two most powerful nations on earth as the only contestants.

President John F. Kennedy let the world know that the United States was fairly dedicated to lunar exploration in his second State of the Union message to Congress on May 25, 1961:

> *"Now is the time to take longer strides — time for a great new American enterprise — time for this nation to take a clearly leading role in space achievement which in many ways may hold the key to our future on Earth —*
>
> *"Recognizing the head start obtained by the Soviets with their large rocket engines . . . we nevertheless are required to make new efforts on our own . . . this is not merely a*

race. Space is open to us now; and our eagerness to share its meaning is not governed by the effort of others. We go into space because whatever mankind must undertake, free men must fully share. . . .

"First, I believe that this Nation should commit itself to achieving the goal, before this decade is out, of landing a man on the Moon and returning him safely to Earth. No single space project in this period will be more impressive to mankind, or more important for the long-range exploration of space; and none will be so difficult or expensive to accomplish. . . . It will not be one man going to the Moon — if we make this judgment affirmatively, it will be an entire nation. . . ."

Since the President and the Congress set the moon landing in this decade as a national goal, the nation's space planners divided the task into three major projects — Mercury, Gemini, and Apollo. Each of these is designed to lay a foundation for future progress.

Project Mercury

PROJECT MERCURY was organized on October 5, 1959. Its objective was to orbit a manned craft about the earth, investigate man's reaction to and abilities in space flight, and recover safely both man and spacecraft. Astronauts Alan B. Shepard, Jr., and Virgil I. Grissom made Mercury suborbital flights on May 5 and July 21, 1961, respectively. Both flew as high as 115 miles above the earth and landed in the Atlantic Ocean about 300 miles from their launch site at Cape Kennedy.

On February 20, 1962, John H. Glenn, Jr., flew three times around the world, thus becoming the first American to orbit the earth. Glenn was followed three months later by M. Scott Carpenter. A few months later, Walter M. Schirra, Jr., made a six-orbit flight. On May 16, 1963, L. Gordon Cooper, Jr., successfully landed after a twenty-two-orbit flight to complete the Mercury program.

The Mercury flights answered many questions for future moon explorers. They demonstrated that men could withstand the high gravity forces of takeoff and entry into the atmosphere, and weightlessness in flight. Just as important, the flights proved that the astronauts could perform tasks in space just as easily as they could in the cockpits of modern jet aircraft. In addition, it was found that they could make observations in space and conduct various experiments without undue difficulty.

Project Gemini

USING THE KNOWLEDGE gained in Project Mercury, American astronauts began Project Gemini. Taking its name from the Greek word meaning "twin," it has four main goals: to determine man's performance and behavior during orbital flights for as long as two weeks; to develop rendezvous and docking techniques; to carry out experiments that require participation and supervision of men aboard the spacecraft; and to demonstrate controlled entry into the atmosphere and landing at a selected site.

The first manned Gemini flight (designated Gemini 3) took place on March 23, 1965. The "Gemini twins," Virgil I. Grissom and John W. Young, orbited the earth for 4 hours and 53 minutes and were the first pilots to steer their craft in flight. Three times during the flight they changed the orbit of their craft by firing tiny engines.

On June 3, 1965, the second manned flight, Gemini 4, blasted off from Cape Kennedy, Florida, with astronauts James A. McDivitt, command pilot, and Edward H. White II, pilot. After 62

Astronaut Edward White II is shown here performing his historic "spacewalk" during the third orbit of the Gemini 4 flight. The first American to egress his spacecraft while in orbit, White remained outside the craft for 21 minutes. (NASA)

revolutions of the earth and 97 hours and 56 minutes of flight, they splashed down in the Atlantic Ocean.

During the third revolution of their flight, Astronaut White left the spacecraft to walk in space, while Astronaut McDivitt remained at the controls. Remaining outside for twenty-one minutes, White took a number of pictures, including the first photograph ever taken of a spacecraft in space from a vantage point outside the spacecraft.

The period of August 21 to 29, 1965, marked an important milestone in the journey to the moon. During those eight days, astronauts L. Gordon Cooper, Jr., and Charles Conrad, Jr., broke a number of existing manned space flight records and established many new ones. Their flight covered 120 revolutions of the earth — a total of 3,312,993 miles — in an elapsed time of 190 hours and 56 minutes.

On December 4, 1965, Gemini 7, with astronauts Frank Borman and James A. Lovell, Jr., aboard, was sent into orbit. They photographed the moon during the next 165 lunar nights and performed many experiments, including shedding their space suits in flight and flying in formation with the detached second phase of the booster.

Eleven days after Gemini 7 had departed for its 14-day, 206-orbit flight, Gemini 6, piloted by astronauts Walter Schirra and Thomas P. Stafford, rocketed into space. Their powerful booster placed them into an elliptical orbit that nearly coincided with that of Gemini 7. Then, by careful maneuvering, Gemini 6 closed slowly with its sister ship until the two spacecraft were only inches apart. For the first time in history, two manned space vehicles flew and maneuvered in formation.

Both Gemini 6 and 7 space crews completed their mission with flawless precision. Besides conducting many medical experiments, the results of which will help future moon travelers, the Gemini 7 crew made many contributions to the other sciences. By using a hand-held sextant to sight stars, they were able to determine their position in space and thus prove that astronauts can navigate without the aid of computers. They also took infrared measurements of the ionized air formed when their craft reentered the earth's atmosphere and communicated with earth stations by use of a laser beam.

In March, 1966, Gemini 8 blasted off with astronauts Neil A. Armstrong and David Scott. After four orbits, the spacecraft rendezvoused and docked with an Agena target vehicle. For the first time, men had joined two craft in space.

The Gemini 8 crew was not able to carry out its full mission and had to abort. Even so, the docking maneuver was a significant accomplishment and proved that it could be done.

Gemini 9, piloted by astronauts Thomas Stafford and Eugene Cernan, was lofted into orbit in June, 1966. It was followed by the Gemini 10 flight the next month, during which astronauts John Young and Mike Collins wrote a bright new chapter in the space handbook. Gemini 10 became the first spaceship ever to use the fuel and propulsion system of another craft for its own power, thereby demonstrating the feasibility of in-space refueling. In addition, the two pilots accomplished a rendezvous with the target vehicle without the use of on-board radar.

Gemini 11 was sent aloft in September, 1966. It demonstrated a tricky first orbit rendezvous with an Agena rocket and thus simulated the Apollo-Lunar Excursion module rendezvous which will come later.

The Last Step — Project Apollo

IT IS PROJECT APOLLO that will be the biggest and most complex of the three major lunar programs. Its goal, to land Americans on the moon and return them to earth, will be accomplished in three steps:

> (1) Earth-orbital flights of up to two weeks' duration so that the crews can gain experience handling the craft and conducting experiments.
> (2) Earth-orbital flights during which crews will learn how to rendezvous and dock with the two-man lunar excursion module.
> (3) Landing of an expedition to explore the moon and return.

PROJECT APOLLO
SPACECRAFT

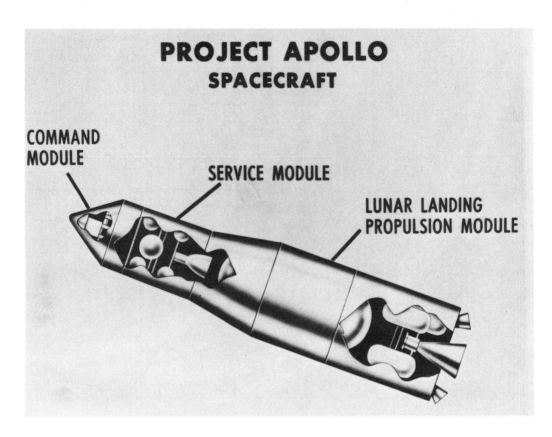

COMMAND MODULE

SERVICE MODULE

LUNAR LANDING PROPULSION MODULE

The three-man Apollo spacecraft will consist of three sections, or modules: a command module, service module, and lunar excursion module. The command module may be likened to the passenger and crew compartments of an airliner. It will be designed so that three men can work, eat, and sleep in it without wearing pressure suits. In addition to life-support equipment, it will contain windows, periscopes, controls, and instrument panels to enable the astronauts to pilot their craft. It may have an airlock to permit a pressure-suited crewman to exit into space. Of the three modules, only the command module will return to earth. Thus, it must be built to withstand the tremendous deceleration forces and intense heating caused by reentry into earth's atmosphere.

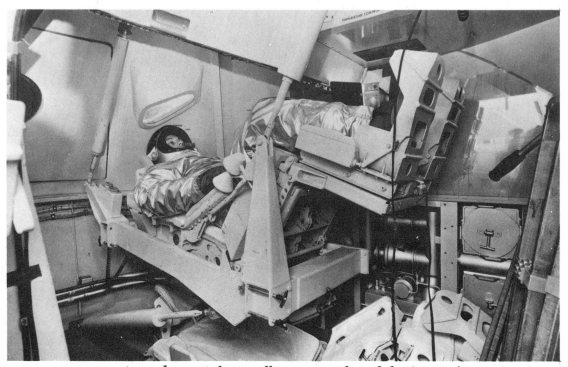

A mock-up of the Apollo command module. (NASA)

The command module will have some maneuverability in the earth's atmosphere, and the pilots will be able to guide their craft toward a predetermined landing area on the moon. The command module will weigh about 5 tons, stand 12 feet tall, and have a base diameter of about 13 feet.

The service module will contain fuel and rockets so that the pilots can propel their craft into and out of lunar orbit and change their course in space. This segment will weigh about 25 tons, and measure 23 feet and be about 13 feet in diameter. It will be jettisoned just before reentry into earth's atmosphere.

The lunar excursion module — informally called the Bug — will be designed for two men to be carried from lunar orbit to the

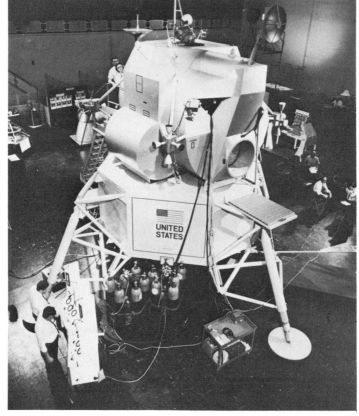

The Lunar Excursion Module (LEM). (NASA)

moon's surface, launched back into lunar orbit, and then reunited with the command and service modules.

When fully fueled and assembled, the Bug will weigh some 12 tons, be about 15 feet high, and have a diameter of about 10 feet. Braking rockets will enable the module to hover while the astronauts survey their landing area, and then enable them to land gently on the moon's surface. Before landing, the excursion module will extend five spider-like legs for support. The legs and landing rocket will support the excursion module in the launch from the moon and then will be left on the moon. When the module itself leaves the moon's surface, it will weigh about 4 tons.

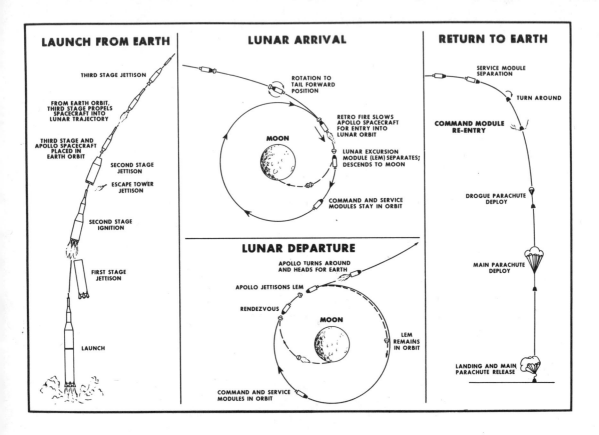

LAUNCH FROM EARTH

THIRD STAGE JETTISON

FROM EARTH ORBIT, THIRD STAGE PROPELS SPACECRAFT INTO LUNAR TRAJECTORY

THIRD STAGE AND APOLLO SPACECRAFT PLACED IN EARTH ORBIT

SECOND STAGE JETTISON

ESCAPE TOWER JETTISON

SECOND STAGE IGNITION

FIRST STAGE JETTISON

LAUNCH

LUNAR ARRIVAL

ROTATION TO TAIL FORWARD POSITION

RETRO FIRE SLOWS APOLLO SPACECRAFT FOR ENTRY INTO LUNAR ORBIT

MOON

LUNAR EXCURSION MODULE (LEM) SEPARATES; DESCENDS TO MOON

COMMAND AND SERVICE MODULES STAY IN ORBIT

LUNAR DEPARTURE

APOLLO TURNS AROUND AND HEADS FOR EARTH

APOLLO JETTISONS LEM

RENDEZVOUS

MOON

LEM REMAINS IN ORBIT

COMMAND AND SERVICE MODULES IN ORBIT

RETURN TO EARTH

SERVICE MODULE SEPARATION

TURN AROUND

COMMAND MODULE RE-ENTRY

DROGUE PARACHUTE DEPLOY

MAIN PARACHUTE DEPLOY

LANDING AND MAIN PARACHUTE RELEASE

Apollo Earth Orbital Missions

IN THE FIRST PHASE of the Apollo project, the command and service modules will be launched into earth orbit by Saturn I, the Free World's largest rocket engine. At launch, the command module will be atop the vehicle, with a rocket-propelled escape tower resembling that on the Mercury spacecraft. The service module will be just below the command module.

The astronauts will remain in space for as long as two weeks before returning to earth. During this time, they will acquire experience in operating their craft and will conduct assigned scientific experiments and observations requiring man's direct participation and supervision.

When a more powerful launch vehicle, the Saturn IB, becomes available, all three modules of the Apollo spacecraft can be launched into earth orbit. At launch, the Bug will be below the service module. In orbit, it will be possible to move the command and service modules around and dock them nose to nose with the Bug. Airlocks will be opened and two of the three astronauts can climb into the Bug.

They will detach the Bug and practice flying it away from the mother craft and then returning the two together. These rehearsals, conducted close to the earth, will enable the astronauts to familiarize themselves with the equipment and to learn the skills that they will need to carry out such operations in the vicinity of the moon. When the maneuvers have been completed, the astronauts will return to the command module, discard the Bug in orbit, and use the service module rocket to change their flight path to one that will bring them safely back to earth.

The Lunar Landing

THE MISSION to the moon will become possible when the enormous power of the Saturn V launch vehicle becomes available. To appreciate the great increase in launch power that is planned, it is best to compare the newer launch vehicles with the Atlas, which was used to launch the Mercury spacecraft.

The Mercury spacecraft weighed about 3,000 pounds. The Saturn I to be used in the first phase of Project Apollo will have the power to lift the equivalent of almost eleven Mercury spacecraft into the same low orbit.

For the landing on the moon, more than ten times the lifting power of the Saturn I is required. The three-stage Saturn V will be able to boost into earth orbit the equivalent weight of eighty Mercury spacecraft.

Together with the three modules of the Apollo spacecraft, the Saturn V will stand about 360 feet tall (longer than a football field), and will weigh about 6 million pounds at launch.

On a lunar landing mission — which may be preceded by one or more flights into deep space and possibly culminate in a flight into lunar orbit and return to earth — the first two stages of the Saturn V and part of the fuel of the third stage will be burned to place the spacecraft and third stage into an earth orbit. At the proper position and time for achieving a lunar trajectory, the third stage will be fired to accelerate the assembly to a speed of about 25,000 miles per hour in the direction of the moon.

Following burnout of the Saturn V third stage, the Apollo crew will disconnect the command and service modules and link the command module nose to nose with the lunar excursion module.

During the flight to the moon, the Apollo astronauts must be ever alert to the threats of dangerous solar flares and other space hazards. In the uncharted blackness of space, they will have to pilot their ship to the moon by taking bearings on stars and other astronomical bodies. They will be aided by navigational and guidance equipment, including a computer, star-seeking devices, and electronic apparatus.

Periodically, they will check their own physical and mental conditions and the condition of every piece of operating equipment on board their craft and make scientific observations. They will report frequently to earth.

When they reach the moon's vicinity, the astronauts will rotate Apollo to a tail-forward position and fire a rocket in the service module to swerve into an approximately 100-mile altitude lunar orbit. As Apollo coasts around the moon, two crewmen will transfer from the command module to the lunar excursion module. The third man will remain in the command module.

The two crewmen will separate their excursion module from the parent craft and fire braking rockets to descend. At low altitude, they will fire their vehicle's tail rockets so that the craft hovers, permitting a final scrutiny of their landing area. At this point, the pilots will be able to rocket their ship back to the parent craft without landing, should they so decide. To land, they will extend their craft's landing gear, five spider-like legs, and vary the motor's thrust for a gentle touchdown.

The astronauts will spend a day or more on the moon, collecting surface samples, taking photographs, examining the lunar surface and moonscape, and performing other scientific experiments. They will radio their reports back to earth, which will be clearly visible to them.

On future missions, the astronauts may lengthen their expedition on the moon. Toward this end, a carrier is being considered which could be launched in advance of Apollo toward the projected landing area. The carrier would contain spare oxygen, food, water, fuel, and perhaps additional scientific instruments.

Upon completing their work, the astronauts will take off and rendezvous in lunar orbit with the parent craft. After they transfer to the command module, the excursion module will be jettisoned. A 22,000-pound-thrust rocket in the service module will then be fired, boosting Apollo from lunar orbit toward earth.

A critical part of this mission is reentry into the earth's atmosphere. At the return speed of 25,000 miles per hour, Apollo must follow an extremely precise flight path called an "entry corridor" to avoid burning up or bouncing back into space. The astronauts will use the service module for propulsion and will maneuver until they are in the entry corridor. Then they will jettison the service module.

The command module will be subjected to extreme stresses and searing heat as the atmosphere slows its headlong flight. At about 60,000 feet, a small parachute called a *drogue* will open and sta-

bilize the craft. At about 10,000 feet above earth, large main parachutes will open and lower the command module gently to a predetermined land area. Recovery forces will race to pick up the astronauts and their spacecraft.

Space flight is now a reality. President John F. Kennedy, the day before he was assassinated, said:

> *"This nation has tossed its cap over the wall of space — and we have no choice but to follow it. Whatever the difficulties, they will be overcome; whatever the hazards, they must be guarded against. With the help of all those who labor in the space endeavor, with the help and support of all Americans, we will climb the wall with safety and with speed — and we shall then explore the wonders of the other side."*

If there were ever any doubt that men would someday go to the moon, that doubt should now be gone. The dream of centuries will soon be realized. Man will not only go to the moon. That will be only the beginning. He will go beyond.

◀ *A model of a small region of the lunar surface, an astronaut, and the Lunar Excursion Module. Scaling technique was based on data transmitted by Ranger 7. (NASA)*

Latin-English Names for the Lunar Seas

Mare Australe	The Southern Sea
Mare Autumni	The Autumn Sea
Mare Crisium	The Sea of Crises
Mare Desiderii	The Sea of Dreams
Pauls Epidemiarum	The Marsh of Epidemics
Mare Fecunditatis	The Sea of Fertility
Mare Frigoris	The Cold Sea
Mare Hiemis	The Winter Sea
Mare Humboldtianum	Humboldt's Sea
Mare Humorum	The Sea of Moisture
Mare Imbrium	The Sea of Showers
Sinus Iridum	The Sea of Rainbows
Mare Marginis	The Marginal Sea
Sinus Medii	The Central Bay
Lacus Mortis	The Lake of Death
Mare Moscoviae	The Sea of Moscow
Palus Nebularum	The Marsh of Mists
Mare Nectaris	The Sea of Nectar
Mare Nubium	The Sea of Clouds
Mare Orientalis	The Eastern Sea
Oceanus Procellarum	The Ocean of Storms
Palus Putredinis	The Marsh of Decay
Mare Serenitatis	The Sea of Serenity
Sinus Aestuum	The Bay of Heats
Mare Smythii	Smyth's Sea
Palus Somnii	The Marsh of Sleep
Lacus Somniorum	The Lake of Dreams
Mare Spumans	The Foaming Sea
Mare Tranquillitatis	The Sea of Tranquility
Mare Undarum	The Sea of Waves
Mare Vaporum	The Sea of Vapors

Moon Statistics

Distance from the Earth	252,710 miles at apogee
	221,463 miles at perigee
	238,857 miles mean distance
Diameter	2,162 miles (¼ the diameter of the earth)
Circumference	6,800 miles
Mass	1/81 of the earth
Volume	1/49 of the earth
Orbital Speed	2,287 miles per hour
Synodic Period	29 days, 12 hours, 44 minutes, 2.8 seconds
Sidereal Period	27 days, 7 hours, 43 minutes, 11.5 seconds
Escape Velocity	1.5 miles per second
Density	3⅓ times density of water (3/5 the density of earth)
Surface Gravity	1/6 the gravity on earth

United States Timetable for Lunar Exploration

Project	Purpose	Schedule
Mercury	Study launching and reentry of space vehicles and the ability of man to live and work in space	Completed in 1963
Ranger	Take detailed photos of the lunar surface and impact of craft on the moon	Completed in 1965
Surveyor	Soft landing on the moon with television cameras; study of lunar surface; scientific experiments	Achieved in 1966
Gemini	Two-man earth-orbiting vehicle to study spacecraft control and space survival for periods up to two weeks	1965–68
Surveyor	Advanced vehicles are planned to make further detailed surveys over extensive areas of the moon	1968–69
Apollo	Manned flights in vicinity of the moon preparatory to landing later	1967–69
Apollo	First landing on the moon	**1969**

Index

78